LIVER AILMENTS AND COMMON DISORDERS

Sound dietary advice on dealing with liver troubles and a variety of other common disorders of the body.

LIVER AILMENTS
AND
COMMON DISORDERS

•

*Prepared and produced by the Editorial Committee
of Science of Life Books*

•

SCIENCE OF LIFE BOOKS
4-12 Tattersalls Lane, Melbourne, Victoria 3000

Fourth (Revised) Edition 1969
Second Impression July 1971
Third Impression May 1972
Fifth Edition, revised and reset, 1975
Second Impression 1977
Third Impression 1981

*Registered at the G.P.O. Sydney
for transmission through the post
as a book*

National Library of Australia card number
and ISBN 0 909911 76 2

Printed in Great Britain by
Richard Clay (The Chaucer Press) Ltd,
Bungay, Suffolk

CONTENTS

LIVER AILMENTS

The liver is one of the most important and vital organs in the body and it functions as the body's chemical laboratory. It is situated on the right side, just under the lower ribs. Its three principal functions are: (1) to produce bile, (2) to store glycogen and (3) to excrete waste products. The liver also renders harmless, certain poisons that may enter the body.

Bile is required to make food alkaline, to emulsify fats and thus assist the digestive processes, and to act as a natural purgative and thereby help in the elimination of waste products from the body.

When the liver releases glycogen, it is converted into glucose, which is the fuel of the body and is 'burned' to give energy. Practically all the food we eat passes through the liver via the great portal vein.

The liver destroys viruses and poisonous bacteria that enter the bloodstream, and it has much to do with the digestion of protein foods, i.e., meat, fish, eggs, cheese and nuts.

Many liver disorders are due to this organ being over-taxed in trying to cope with an excess of protein foods.

What to avoid

The usual treatment of liver ailments is with drugs such as calomel, which are most injurious to the liver. Such drugs force the liver into unnatural activity which, instead of improving that organ, may leave it exhausted and often injured.

The main causes of liver trouble can be summed up briefly: over-eating; excess of protein and starchy food; too much rich, greasy, mixed, messy and fried foods; the use of devitalized and dead foods; the use of condiments, sauces, seasonings, spices, and too much salt; over-indulgence in alcoholic drinks; the use of pills and medicine to 'shake up' the liver; lack of exercise.

Jaundice

Jaundice is not a disease, but the symptom of one. It is due to a blockage of the common duct leading from the gall-bladder to the duodenum. The flow of bile is held up and the bile is passed into the blood instead of into the digestive system.

The cause of the obstruction may be a gall-stone (see later reference to gall-stones) or a catarrhal or inflammatory condition, or a tumour. The bile is greenish-yellow in colour. Its entry into the bloodstream gives the sufferer a characteristic yellow colour, and the whites of the eyes become particularly affected.

Recommendations: Stop all food with the exception of diluted citrus fruit juices as long as the acute symptoms last – usually three to seven days. After that the patient should be put on a fruit and salad vegetable diet for a few days. The bowels should be cleansed each night with an enema of warm water. As the patient gets stronger the diet of fresh fruit and vegetables may also include cheese and eggs, wheatgerm and milk. The following vitamins should be taken before meals, three times daily:

1 Vitamin A tablet (750 i.u.'s), 1 Vitamin B1

tablet (10 mg), 2 Vitamin B12 tablets, 1 Folic Acid tablet, 1 Vitamin B-complex tablet, 1 Vitamin E tablet (50 mg), 1 Vitamin C (250 mg) tablet, 1 Kelp tablet.

(Where a tumour or gall-stones are concerned, an operation may be necessary.)

Cirrhosis of the Liver

This complaint cripples the liver. It develops when the liver has been required to cope with enormous quantities of poisonous materials and has become prematurely worn-out.

Relief must be given the liver by taking diluted citrus fruit juices and avoiding all food excesses, particularly fats, since the digestion of fats throws much work upon the liver. Meat, condiments, and alcoholic beverages must be avoided. Copious water drinking is recommended. If bile is lacking, bile salts may have to be given. The following vitamins should be taken three times a day, before meals:

1 Vitamin A tablet, 2 Vitamin B12 (25 mg) tablets, 1 Folic Acid (5 mg) tablet, 1 Vitamin C tablet (250 mg), 1 Vitamin B1 (10 mg) tablet, 1 Vitamin B-complex tablet, 1 Kelp tablet, 1 Vitamin E tablet (50 mg).

Hepatitis

This is an infectious complaint and is characterized by high temperature, headache, abdominal discomfort and loss of appetite. Usually, six to eight weeks are required for recovery, but the worst symptoms disappear much earlier. Its cause is due to a virus and it is known to be spread by houseflies and unclean personal habits. Unsewered areas are likely to have a high incidence of hepatitis unless precautions are taken.

Serum heptatitis can result from blood transfusions and from dental and medical injections. Hepatitis has also been attributed to tattooing operations. Some authorities consider that there is a connection between the use of D.D.T. and the incidence of hepatitis.

In the early stages the diet should be of diluted citrus juices only. Later, puréed fruits and vegetables may be given, but fats should be used sparingly, and salt must not be taken.

The following vitamins should be taken three times a day, before meals:

1 Vitamin A tablet, (750 i.u.'s), 1 Vitamin E tablet (50 mg.), 1 Vitamin B1 tablet (10 mg), 1 Vitamin B-complex tablet, 1 Vitamin C tablet (250 mg), 2 Vitamin B12 tablets, 1 Folic Acid tablet (5 mg) and 1 Kelp tablet.

Gall-bladder Trouble

It has been said that one adult in five may eventually have gall-stones, and at least half the women over sixty will have them.

The gall-bladder reposes under the right lobe of the liver and its job is to store bile, a greenish yellow or golden brown bitter fluid, required to emulsify and absorb fats, also to stimulate intestinal function and encourage the digestive action of the pancreatic juice.

The liver is constantly making bile, which is held in the gall-bladder until fats have to be assimilated, when bile is discharged directly into the duodenum (the exit from stomach to intestines).

What happens to those whose gall-bladders have been removed? The bile ducts, narrow tubes that lead from the liver to the gall-bladder and from the latter to the duodenum, enlarge, so that more bile can flow through them, and some bile is apparently stored there. This arrangement is, of course, not nearly so efficient, so it is advisable to retain your gall-bladder, if possible, by ensuring that it is kept healthy.

Gall-stones

When there has been neglect, one or more gall-stones become lodged in the bile duct that connects the gall-bladder and intestines. The entire process of digestion then becomes obstructed and jaundice follows, and unless the stone or stones pass through the bile duct, surgery is essential.

According to Adelle Davis, the famous American nutrition expert, experiments and laboratory animals have revealed that those 'whose diets are adequate in all respects except for sufficient vitamin A, are especially susceptible to infections . . . Almost ninety per cent of the animals develop stones in the bladder, kidneys, or gall-bladder.'

Gall-stones are composed principally of cholesterol, found in the bile, and it is significant that those with gall-stones generally eat more than they should of fatty animal foods rich in cholesterol, such as butter, fat bacon, and other fatty meats, eggs, etc.

Importance of Vitamins B and C

When the diet lacks the B group of vitamins, normal energy flags, and the contractions of the walls of the gall-bladder become feeble, and may cease altogether.

The bile is not then emptied from the gall-bladder and the cholesterol, being a heavy, waxy substance, settles in the gall-bladder to form gall-stones.

It is also considered that a lack of vitamin C is responsible to some degree for the formation of gall-stones.

Overweight

A warning note has also been sounded to the effect that gall-stones can be induced by the near starvation diets that some people resort to in an attempt to lose weight.

We may summarize by saying that the principal characteristic of gall-bladder sufferers is overweight. The same fatty foods that cause this, also give them gall-bladder trouble. If we examine their diet it will be found deficient in vitamins A, B-complex, B1 (thiamin), C and E.

Overweight people are advised to read the book *How to Lose Weight and Gain Health*.

Remedial Principles

The following should be taken three times daily after meals for gall-stones and gall-bladder infection:

1 Vitamin A tablet (750 i.u.'s), 1 Vitamin B-complex tablet, 1 Vitamin B1 tablet (10 mg), 1 Vitamin C tablet (250 mg), 1 Vitamin E tablet (50 mg), 2 Vitamin B12 tablets, 1 Choline capsule (250 mg).

Fatty foods should be restricted and emphasis placed upon wheatgerm, fruit, salad vegetables, and lean meat.

MIGRAINE

Migraine has both physical and psychological causes. The traditional diet has much to answer for with its dead, constipating foods and its emphasis upon sugary, starchy and fatty meals.

A migraine attack – also known as a 'bilious attack' – indicates that the digestive system has reached the end of its toxic toleration.

The poisoned condition of the blood, intensified by many aspirin tablets, A.P.C. powders and other drugs intended to stave off the impending attack, inevitably results in dilation of the frontal, temporal or occipital arteries of the brain and gives rise to the worst possible type of headache . . . the completely prostrating type, accompanied by vomiting attacks, visual disturbances and intolerance of light, noise, and movement.

With migraine sufferers there is mostly some weakness of the muscular tissue around the back of the neck, which gives rise to tension. The scalp muscles too, are subject to tension.

Manipulation of the head and neck can often ward off an attack of migraine and we advise neck and scalp massage regularly, twice a day. This should take the form of rolling the head limply around the neck, in a full circle, stretching and massaging the neck with the hands and massaging the scalp, especially around the back of the neck.

These exercises will strengthen the nerves and blood vessels which ramify from the top of the spine to the head.

The Migraine Type

The migraine sufferer is usually the over-conscientious type, whose worries react so adversely upon his digestive fluids that their secretion is often retarded and food remains undigested. Vomiting affords the only relief. Being a worrier, the blood pressure rises and sets up dilation of the blood vessels of the brain, and the splitting headache that follows it.

Migraine attacks are frequently triggered-off by such emotional disturbances as anxiety, frustration or resentment, or from over-fatigue, exposure or eye-strain, but most migraine sufferers have a history of dietetic excesses, indiscretions and constipation, all of which contribute to the building up of a migraine attack.

The basic solution of the problem of migraine lies in a simple vital diet, free from second-rate and complicated concoctions which masquerade as 'food' in so many food shops today . . . particularly the delicatessen, confectionery and cake shops.

If the migraine attack has already developed and is causing distress, take hot footbaths and apply cold compresses to the base of the skull and neck. It is frequently beneficial to lie in a bath of water at a temperature around bloodheat for half an hour or so. Allow the water to cool slowly, but do not become chilled.

Remedial Principles

The following should be taken three times daily, before meals:

1 Fort-E-Plex tablet, 2 Yogurt tablets, 1 Vitamin B1 tablet (10 mg), 2 Calcium (white) tablets, 3

Vitamin B12 tablets.

On retiring:

1 Fort-E-Plex tablet, 2 Calcium tablets (white).
The diet should consist mainly of vital foods, such as fresh fruits, salads, 'short-cooked' vegetables, wheatgerm, cheese, brewer's yeast, nuts and milk.

Vitamin B Deficiencies

The pyschological aspect of migraine comes under the heading of psychosomatic illness, and it is maintained that a deficiency of the B group of vitamins contributes towards a person becoming readily upset emotionally. Consequently it is necessary to be sure that a sufferer's diet is adequate in all respects, but particularly with regard to the B-complex vitamins.

It goes without saying, of course, that all vitamins are important for the maintenance of the health of the migraine sufferer, just as for others, and a balanced diet which provides adequate daily requirements is an absolute necessity. On top of this vitamin B supplements can be taken, and a 10 mg tablet of vitamin B1 before each meal, and on retiring, is beneficial.

Migraine and 'Sugar Starvation'

According to recent medical research, many sufferers from migraine are victims of 'sugar starvation,' and there is a close link with the latter condition and the attacks characteristic of the ailment.

Sugar starvation, or low blood sugar (known medically as hyper-insulinism) can best be explained by stating that all the food we eat is ultimately converted by the chemistry of the body into glucose or blood sugar . . . not to be confused with cane sugar or commercial glucose. To 'burn' the blood sugar, insulin is essential. Insulin is secreted by a special group of cells in the pancreas. When, for some reason that is not yet clear, but which seems likely to be due to vitamin deficiencies, this special group of cells becomes over-active, too much insulin is produced which burns up the blood sugar so rapidly that the body is left without energy, and a feeling of weakness and depression is experienced. It is at such periods, when the level of the blood sugar is at its lowest, that a bodily condition is set up favourable to migraine attacks.

Need for 'Midmeals'

The old idea that 'eating between meals is bad for you' does not apply to those with blood sugar starvation. On the contrary, they are advised to eat 'midmeals' at, say, 11 a.m., 4 p.m. and 9 p.m., to prevent the level of the blood sugar falling too low between ordinary meals.

Dr E.M. Abrahamson, in *Body, Mind and Sugar*, states that midmeals must be of proteins only, or of fruits and fruit juices, and must *not* include any starchy or sugary foods. He considers they should be light and consist of, for example, a glass of milk, or a glass of fruit or vegetable juice. Alternatively, a midmeal can be made of a piece of cheese, a few nuts, or a piece of fruit, so long as the fruit is not excessively sugary (dates, dried fruits, raisins, bananas, grapes, figs, plums, peaches and apricots should *not* be eaten for midmeals).

Dr Abrahamson's discoveries about hyper-insulinism are confirmed by other leading medical men, including B.P. Sandler, M.D., C.F. Wilkinson, M.D., J.A. Harrill, M.D., and Dr Searle Harris, Professor of Medicine at the University of Alabama, U.S.A.

Sufferers from migraine are advised to adopt the ideas of Dr Abrahamson regarding a reduced intake of sugar and starchy foods, also to take midmeals of proteins, as well as the vitamins we have mentioned. Migraine sufferers are also recommended to avoid salty foods and to cut down their use of table salt to a minimum.

KIDNEY AND BLADDER TROUBLES

The kidneys are situated on each side of the spine, at the back of the abdomen. Their principal functions are to excrete urea and uric acid, salts and other waste products, and filter excess water from the blood, which is discharged as urine into the bladder and thence from the body. About 4,000 quarts of fluid pass through the kidneys every day.

The kidneys form a most remarkable filtration plant, the entire length of tubules or tiny tubes in both kidneys being about 280 miles. Each kidney is provided with several million nephrons or renal units, the whole being compressed into a space of about 20 cubic inches. All the blood in the body flows through the kidneys every few minutes.

How Kidney Trouble Arises
A potent cause of kidney trouble is a dietary in which

meat, fish, eggs, cheese and other high protein foods
are over-indulged in, together with an excess of
devitalized starchy and sugary foods, also fats. These
foods impose a great strain upon the kidneys, which
are required to dispose of the body's toxic wastes.
Such foods tend to replace in the modern diet, salad
vegetables, which should be served *with* proteins to
obtain a proper balance. More fruit should also be
eaten at meals.

Kidney troubles mostly appear when the sufferer is
beginning to get on in years. It usually takes some
time for the kidneys to break down and for kidney
diseases to appear, but previous drug treatment for
fevers, influenza, pneumonia and other acute diseases,
causes serious injury to the kidneys, and often sets up
permanent kidney weakness. The continual use of
aspirin, antacid powders and A.P.C. powders is
harmful to the kidneys.

Danger of Drugs

Many chemical substances are most difficult for the
kidneys to excrete. When sodium bicarbonate and
antacid powders are taken to relieve heartburn and
indigestion, for example, a residue of chemical matter
remains in the stomach. It is ultimately carried by the
bloodstream to the kidneys, which have difficulty in
disposing of such residue.

With advancing years, the kidneys find it
increasingly difficult to cope with such chemicals,
which irritate the sensitive kidney structure. The same
remarks apply to A.P.C. powders, aspirin, phenacetin,
phenobarbital, sulpha drugs, 'wonder' drugs and
antibiotics, practically all of which have drastic results
upon the kidneys, as well as neutralizing the vitamins

in the body. The use of strong tea and coffee free use of condiments, salt and salty foods, spiced foods and alcoholic beverages, all have an adverse effect upon the proper working of the kidneys.

Bright's Disease or Nephritis

The causes of this complaint have already been discussed, namely a toxic bloodstream arising from a devitalized diet with (frequently) faulty elimination. Bright's disease is often precipitated by a chill or exposure.

Remedial Principles: The diet should consist only of diluted citrus fruit juices during the acute period. Later, the food should be free from salt. For the first two or three weeks the protein intake should be greatly restricted. Milk may be given, also fruit, fruit and vegetable juices, salads, wheatgerm, a little cheese and a small quantity of wheatmeal bread, but no meat, fish or eggs.

The following vitamins are essential for speedy recovery and should be taken three times a day before food:

1 Vitamin A tablet (750 i.u.'s), 1 Vitamin B-complex tablet, 1 Vitamin C tablet (250 mg), 1 Safflower Oil, Lecithin or Sunflower Oil capsule and 1 Vitamin E capsule or tablet (100 mg). If there is high blood-pressure, only one vitamin E capsule should be taken daily, instead of three.

Cystitis (Inflammation of the Bladder)

This complaint is secondary to kidney trouble and arises when the bladder lining becomes inflamed after the continued passage of infected urine from diseased kidneys. The urine infects the ureters and the urethra as well as the bladder, making urination frequent and painful.

Remedial Principles: The diet, vitamin therapy and dosage should be as advised for Bright's Disease.

Pyelitis (Inflammation of the Renal Pelvis)

This ailment is generally caused by toxic bacteria in the bloodstream, resulting in the formation of pus in the kidneys and ureters. Sometimes the pain associated with the condition is the result of gravel or kidney stones.

Remedial Principles: The diet, vitamin therapy and dosage should be as advised for Bright's Disease. Severe cases of Pyelitis may require penicillin, but mild chronic cases usually respond to a diet which while purifying the bloodstream, also takes the strain off the kidneys.

Kidney Stone (Urinary or Renal Calculi)

Stone in the kidney or bladder is a very painful affliction, especially when the stone is being passed from the kidney to the bladder on its way down the ureter, or through the tube leading from the bladder, i.e., the urethra.

Kidney stones are mostly formed of crystals of phosphate or oxalate of lime, which are precipitated out of the urine whilst in the kidneys or bladder. The presence of these toxic products cleary indicates that the blood has become clogged with impurities through unwise feeding habits.

An operation for remove of the stone may be necessary, but it must be realized that stones may again form unless the faulty diet is greatly improved. In experiments with animals, laboratory tests have proved that kidney stones ('gravel') have been produced when the animals' diets have been deficient in vitamin A, and that the stones have disappeared when vitamin A is added. People with kidney stones require one vitamin A capsule of 750 i.u.'s after each meal.

In kidney stone trouble, vitamins C and E are also important. Vitamin C in massive dosage prevents uric acid sediment from calcifying – that is, forming into tiny stones or silting up in the joints. Vitamin E is necessary for all kidney troubles because it greatly improves the circulation of the blood. The kidneys are a vital part of the circulatory mechanism, the blood passing through the filtrate network of the kidneys every few minutes, as we have already pointed out. Vitamin E also strengthens the muscular tissue forming the kidneys, and aids in the repair of kidney injuries.

The diet, vitamin therapy and dosage for kidney stones are the same as for Bright's Disease.

Haematuria (Blood in the Urine)
This may be due to one of several causes. It is generally the result of disease or injury, either to the kidneys, ureters, urethra or bladder. The passage of a stone from the kidneys can produce haematuria, and certain poisonous drugs can also bring about this condition. Haematuria may also occur in the 'crisis' period of fevers.

This ailment may, or may not be serious, depending upon what has caused it. The diet, vitamin therapy and dosage are as recommended for Bright's Disease.

Bed-wetting (Enuresis)
The child should not partake of liquids within $2\frac{1}{2}$

hours of going to bed. His bed clothing must be adequate but not too heavy. He should be made to empty his bladder just before going to bed, and be awakened two or three hours after and required to urinate again.

The parts in the region of the bladder should be sponged morning and night with cold water, which has a tonic and strengthening effect upon the bladder.

The child should be encouraged to take part in outdoor games.

Remedial Principles: 'The Summary' issued by the Shute Foundation for Medical Research of Canada (Vol. 4, No. 2), states that vitamin E has been used with success in Germany for bed-wetting. This vitamin has a strengthening and beneficial action upon muscular tissue.

Need for Calcium and Vitamins

The rapid growth of children makes a heavy demand upon their body's calcium supply for bone formation. Calcium is, however, also needed to enable both nerves and muscles to relax. A lack of calcium leads to tenseness and irritability, which frequently manifests in tantrums, biting of finger nails, restless sleep and bed-wetting. A teaspoonful of honey at bedtime will often prevent bed-wetting.

The growing child also needs a relatively large amount of B-complex vitamins (so frequently lacking in the ordinary diet). The process of growth added to the child's natural activity, depletes these vitamins. Any shortage of B-complex vitamins results in nerve trouble, lack of endurance, and weakness that will aggravate the bladder difficulty.

The following should be given twice daily before

meals:

> 1 Vitamin E tablet (50 mg), 1 Vitamin B-complex tablet, 2 Calcium tablets (white), and 1 Safflower oil, Sunflower oil or Lecithin capsule.

Recent medical research indicates that in kidney and bladder ailments, the diet has lacked essential unsaturated fatty acids (lecithin).

THE GLANDS AND HEALTH

The glands are defined by *Blakiston's Medical Dictionary*, as 'cells, tissues or organs which elaborate and discharge substances that are used elsewhere in the body, or are eliminated therefrom.'

The glands are nourished by the bloodstream, as it is from the blood that the glands obtain those materials from which they elaborate the various secretions that are utilized by the body. It follows that if the blood is unhealthy, due to faulty nutrition and vitamin and mineral deficiency, this condition may be reflected in glandular disturbances, which can lead to illnesses of a serious nature.

There are secreting glands with ducts, and glands of secretion without ducts. The latter are known as ductless glands or the endocrine system of glands. The secreting glands with ducts include the salivary glands, the tear glands and also that important gland known as the liver, which is the largest gland in the body.

The Lymphatic Glands

The lymphatic glands are placed at strategic points in the body to act as filters of the blood plasma. These glands also perform the vital task of removing poisonous substances from the blood. Examples of the lymphatic glands are the tonsils, the lymphatic glands in the neck, at the back of the nose, under the armpits, and in the groin. The appendix is also a lymphatic gland.

The Spleen

The spleen is located just below the diaphragm, on the left side. This organ is difficult to classify as it has many and diverse functions, relating to the liver, the blood and the circulation. Its chief functions are concerned with the blood. For example, it is a reservoir for red blood cells; it promotes the formation of blood cells; it plays a part in the body's defences against infection, e.g., malaria and typhoid fever. The spleen also destroys degenerate red corpuscles, setting free the bilirubin (red bile pigment) and iron.

The Endocrine Glands

The ductless or endocrine glands secrete hormones or chemical messengers that are discharged directly into the bloodstream to be carried to various organs, to stimulate action. (The word 'hormone' means 'to excite.')

We now deal with the endocrine glands in detail.

The Pituitary Gland

This gland is located at the base of the brain and is connected to the brain by a hollow stem. The pituitary gland is no bigger than a pea, yet it performs several vitally important functions. It consists of an anterior lobe and a posterior lobe.

The hormones produced by its anterior lobe regulate the growth of all bodily tissues, control the development and function of the thyroid gland, the adrenal cortex, the gonads and the parathyroids. They also induce lactation. The activity of the posterior lobe of the pituitary gland affects the blood-pressure, contractility of smooth muscle, and the proper functioning of the kidneys. Other functions of this amazing gland are the control of the mechanism of menstruation, and the protection of the unborn child until birth occurs.

If the anterior lobe of the pituitary gland becomes over-active, the growth of the body is no longer symmetrical, and some parts grow enormously. The hands, feet and lower jaw expand out of all proportion to the rest of the body. This ailment is known as acromegaly. If, on the other hand, the anterior lobe becomes sluggish, resulting in a deficiency of the growth hormone, a form of dwarfism results.

Hirsutism, or an excessive growth of hair in areas not usually hairy, sometimes occurs in women and children, when the pituitary or the adrenal glands are not functioning properly.

The pituitary directs the activity of all the other glands just as a conductor controls an orchestra. Its importance seems to have been recognized by nature for it has been given the seat of honour in the centre of the brain.

The Parathyroid Glands

These four tiny glands are located in the neck at the back of the thyroid gland. Their task is to regulate the calcium mechanism of the body. If one's diet is too low in calcium, this mineral will be withdrawn from the bones and serious bone disease may result. Paget's Disease and Recklinghausen's Disease are considered to be due to faulty functioning of the parathyroid glands.

The Adrenal Glands

These glands (sometimes referred to as the super-renals) are a pair of small glands about the size of a bean, one of which is located on top of each kidney.

The adrenal glands consist of two parts, the outer or cortex, and the inner or medulla. The medulla secretes adrenalin, which stimulates the sympathetic nervous system, has a tonic effect upon the muscles of the heart and the arteries, assists in keeping the blood pressure normal, and also stimulates the bronchi and the muscles.

The cortex is related to the gonads. Tumours of the cortex lead to premature sex development in the male, and sex reversal in the female, especially facial hair and general appearance.

An important feature of the secretion from the medulla is that it causes the body starch, or glycogen, stored in the liver and muscles, to be converted into blood sugar for immediate use as energy. Whenever you are under any kind of stress, be it anger, fright, pain, heat, cold or fatigue, adrenalin is released into the blood to aid you.

Vitamin C is Essential

Healthy adrenal glands need a high concentration of vitamin C, more than is contained in any other part of the body, and any lack of this vitamin reacts badly upon the adrenal glands.

There is a disease of the adrenal cortex called Addison's Disease which results in loss of weight and strength, with a dark pigmentation of the skin. This disease is due to a deficiency of the hormone normally supplied by the adrenal cortex. Another disease known as Cushing's Disease is due to tumours forming on the adrenal cortex.

The Pancreas

This organ is located behind the stomach and extends from the duodenum to the spleen. The pancreas has a dual function. It consists of some cells that secrete pancreatic juice, which contains three enzymes needed in the digestive process. These enzymes have a specific action in promoting a chemical change without themselves being changed.

Insulin and its Function

There is also within the pancreas a specialized group of cells whose task it is to secrete the hormone known as insulin. This group of cells bears the name of 'The islets of Langerhans' after their discoverer. Insulin is needed to 'burn' the blood sugar and thus convert it into energy. When the specialized cells mentioned become over-active, too much insulin is released and the blood sugar is burned too rapidly, resulting in a condition known as low blood sugar or blood sugar 'starvation'. This condition gives rise to chronic fatigue and often to migraine, as we have previously stated.

If too *little* insulin is released, the blood sugar is not burned up quickly enough; it accumulates dangerously and the urine becomes loaded with it.

This is a serious condition and is known as diabetes.

The Thymus Gland

The thymus gland is situated in the chest, just behind the top of the breast-bone. Its purposes and functions are not clear.

The association of thymoma, a primary tumour of the thymus, with the serious neuro-muscular disease known as Myasthenia Gravis, is sufficiently frequent to warrant investigation of the thymus in all cases of Myasthenia Gravis.

There is a theory that the thymus gland in some way controls sex development up to the stage of adolescence, when the sex glands or gonads begin to assume importance, and this might well be true.

Status thymicolymphaticus is a condition in which the thymus persists in adolescence, together with a general increase of lymphoid tissue all over the body. These people readily die under an anaesthetic or from trivial causes, for no known reason. It is impossible to diagnose the condition beforehand.

The Pineal Gland

This gland, about the size of a cherry stone, is situated in the brain. Like the thymus, little is known positively of its functions. No special hormone has been isolated from it. It is thought to be concerned with metabolism, i.e., the synthesizing of foodstuffs into complex tissue elements, and of breaking down complex substances into simple ones, in the production of energy.

The thyroid gland is discussed later in the section headed 'Thyroid Deficiency and Goitre'.

Value of Vitamins

In his popular book *The Glands of Destiny* Dr Ivo Geikie Cobb states that the relationship between the endocrine organs and vitamins is of great importance, and that it would seem that an inadequate supply of vitamins results in a degree of failure in the endocrine system as a whole.

He also points out that ready-prepared foods have in modern times tended to oust the more natural dietary of man. Raw vegetables, fresh fruit and salads have had to take second place to less natural creations of the culinary art, and puddings of a 'poultice-like' consistency have been favoured as being more filling at the price than such health giving items as apples, oranges and bananas.

Dr Cobb lays emphasis on the growing child's need for uncooked fruit and vegetables in abundance if he or she is to be sure of a sufficient intake of vitamins, a clean intestine and a less spotty complexion. He also declares that there is little doubt that the right diet can go a long way to sorting out minor endocrine disturbances, and this is just as applicable to adults as to children.

Proper Nutrition

We cannot emphasize too much the fact, now definitely established by nutritional and endocrine science, that glandular deficiencies can be corrected and inefficient glandular functioning can be remedied. Proper nutrition holds the answer to the problem.

Prof. E.V. McCollum, the famous U.S. nutritional scientist, whose research into the subject is recognized the world over, made this important statement in the course of a letter to Lawrence Armstrong, of

Melbourne:

'The study of gland feeding has always been comparable in my mind to the study of navigation. Just as the constellations guide the seafarer along his unerring path, so does the condition of the endocrine glands give to the skilled observer an unfailing indication of any dietary deficiencies, together with the course which must be charted for a safe arrival at the haven of perfect physical and mental strength.

'Our experience in research work has shown us beyond the slightest shadow of a doubt, that accessory feeding (with vitamins) with a view to revitalizing these delicate organs, is the rational short cut to the desired end.'

You Can Feed Your Glands

As we have already pointed out, the glands draw the substances for their marvellously potent secretions *from the blood*. Your glands are only as healthy as your bloodstream. If the blood becomes impoverished through faulty nutrition, resulting in lack of essential vitamins and minerals, the glands have not the wherewithal to manufacture their secretions to the standards required by a healthy body. Glandular disturbances can then result, leading to the serious gland diseases we have mentioned.

Dr Gayelord Hauser, eminent American nutritional scientist, says in his book *Diet Does It*:

'Each of the glands depends upon our very own bloodstream for its nourishment ... There is a generally popular opinion that if glandular abnormalities occur, they are likely to continue throughout life. Nothing could be further from the truth. If the diet is completely adequate, many glandular abnormalities can be corrected.'

Vitals Foods are Essential

If you would avoid glandular disturbances, or if you are already suffering from such trouble, it would be wise to include in your daily diet such vital, health-giving foods as fruit, salad vegetables, wheatgerm, cheese, honey, milk, nuts, dried fruits, molasses and brewer's yeast, omitting such dead and devitalized foods as white bread, white flour products (such as biscuits and pastry), sugar, jam, fried foods, processed and flaked cereals, condiments, vinegar, soft drinks sweets, polished rice, sausage meats, pies and puddings, and all forms of drugs, aspirin, sleeping pills, etc.

Sufferers from glandular diseases are recommended to take the following, three times daily before meals. (They may be taken together.)

1 Vitamin A tablet (750 i.u.'s), 1 Vitamin B-complex tablet, 1 Vitamin B1 tablet (10 mg), 1 Vitamin C tablet (250 mg), 1 Vitamin E tablet (50 mg), 1 Kelp tablet, 2 Calcium tablets(white), 1 Safflower Oil, Sunflower Oil or Lecithin capsule.

ENLARGED TONSILS AND ADENOIDS

The lymphoid tissues at the back of the soft palate, just above the entrance to the throat, are a ready source of infection in young and old.

Tonsillitis is an inflamed condition of the tonsils,

arising from a toxic or 'run down' condition of the system. A cold or chill often lowers the body's resistance and the infection settles in these soft lymphoid tissues.

Usually the condition quickly clears up if the person affected is put to bed, kept warm, and given frequent drinks of diluted orange and lemon juice (or pineapple juice) with one 250 mg vitamin C tablet, and one vitamin B-complex tablet, three times a day.

As a rule, the patient wants little food, and this should be limited to soup, with a generous flavouring of yeast (or yeast extract), or a little ice-cream. As soon as normal meals are served, a vitamin A capsule should be given with the other vitamins mentioned later.

Should Tonsils be Removed?

Not so long ago the removal of a child's tonsils was almost regarded as a 'fashionable' operation, and at the first sign of trouble parents would be anxious for their doctor to arrange for a tonsillectomy, as the operation is known. And, in most cases the child would go into hospital, the 'offending' tonsils would be surgically removed, and everybody was happy – or at leat thought they were.

Current thinking, however, tends more towards the conviction that tonsillectomy should be regarded as the last resort when all else has failed, and as such is very much in line with nature cure views. Both the tonsils and adenoids stand as protective organs at the main entrance to the body, and an operation serves only to annihilate these important sentries; removing the effects of the infection and not the cause. Only proper diet, regular elimination and general good health can put right the root cause of the problem.

In *Health Via Food*, Dr Wm Howard Hay wrote: 'No one knows the function of the tonsil, or of the appendix, but that these have a definite function is evident for two reasons: one, that they are respectively placed at the gateway and termination of digestion; the other reason is that no one is ever quite so well after their removal as before, as witness the thousands who will tell you so after the removal of these little organs.'

Since then research has proved that the tonsils are important lymphatic glands which have been placed at the entrance to the body to trap noxious bacteria and to prevent it from penetrating deeper – into the bronchia for example.

The tonsils stand guard at the entrance to the body, and are thus in a most vulnerable position. Their role is to bear the brunt of invading infections, to localize them, and to render them harmless. With good health and sound treatment infections of tonsils and adenoids quickly clear up. A significant comment by an English school medical officer, Dr H.M. Keith, is worth quoting. He said: 'I notice that if for any reason an operation advised some time ago has not been done, in many cases it is no longer required.' A warning indeed to think twice when a decision is called for which will determine the fate of a child's tonsils.

A doctor, writing in *Today's Health*, said: 'Nowadays we realize that tonsils are part of the system of lymphatics, with the important job of catching, destroying and disposing of infection before it can go any deeper into the system. Most of the germs we take in come through the throat and nose, so swollen and inflamed tonsils are not necessarily 'infected'. They may instead only be indicating that they are doing their job of trapping infections and helping to build immunity for the future.'

Apparently no one has been able to show statistically that colds, sore throats and other disorders of the breathing apparatus *are less frequent after the tonsils are removed*. In fact, the evidence appears to show that individuals who never had their tonsils out have fewer such infections. This seems reasonable, since the tonsils are there to protect against infection.

Furthermore, it seems important to remember that the body makes every effort to replace the tonsil tissue after it has been removed, for in many cases it grows back again most persistently and stubbornly.

The tonsils are present at birth and grow larger until about the age of three to five, after which the size of the tonsils themselves is gradually reduced and *adenoids disappear almost completely*. So it must not be assumed, because the tonsils of a child this age seem large, that they are therefore harmful – they are naturally large at this age.

Dr Jan Stewer asks in *The Lancet*, 'Do we really know what ill health can be caused by the tonsils? When they are inflamed how does one know whether the infection is endogenous (from within the body) or exogenous (from without)?

'Repeated attacks are taken as evidence of the endogenous infection, but is this true? There's no difficulty in finding children whose recurrent infections are just as common *after* operation as before; the only difference is they have tonsillitis when they have tonsils, or pharyngitis, bronchitis or pneumonia when they haven't. It's just possible that the tonsils are there to prevent their having bronchitis or pneumonia!'

Tonsil Operations and Polio

One important aspect of tonsil removal has been pointed out by the medical profession and that is the grave danger of polio especially if the tonsils are removed during polio season. Many medical articles have warned of this danger, for the polio contracted after tonsillectomies is generally the most serious kind – *bulbar polio*.

Numerous writers in medical journals today plead for prevention rather than operation. In general they suggest the use of antibiotics to treat infected tonsils. We recommend instead a programme of good nutrition. We know well that vitamins A and C protect against infections, and vitamin B strengthens the nervous system.

Drs Bicknell and Prescott, in their monumental book, *The Vitamins in Medicine* tell us that the duration of an attack of tonsillitis in adolescents treated with vitamin C is less than in children who did not receive the vitamin.

Dr J.W.S. Lundahl, writing in *The Practitioner*, declares that 'acute tonsillitis results from a combination of infection and lowered resistance, local and general.

'Measures should therefore be taken to improve the general health. It has been suggested that one predisposing factor, is an unbalanced ·diet with too much sugar and starch in relation to protein and green vegetables, and I believe that there is much to be said for this theory.'

The Adenoids

What we have said about the tonsils and their healthy maintenance, applies equally to the adenoids; those lymphoid structures in the nasopharynx (near the back of the throat). Adenoids are also known as pharyngeal tonsils and their function – like that of the tonsils proper – is one of protecting the child's health. As previously pointed out, adenoids disappear almost completely when they have fulfilled their purpose in the child's life.

Remedial Principles

Usually, any person who is subject to tonsillitis can build up his resistance to infection, and reduce the frequency of attack by the vital dietetic principles set out in this book.

These dietetic principles, fortified with fresh pineapple juice and diluted citrus drinks daily, plus one Vitamin A tablet (750 i.u.'s), one 250 mg Vitamin C tablet and one B-complex tablet, three times a day, before meals, provide the best preventative and also remedial measure.

THYROID DEFICIENCY AND GOITRE

The thyroid gland consists of two lobes, one on each side of the windpipe at the base of the neck. The gland secretes and discharges into the blood stream a potent hormone called 'thyroxin', of which iodine is an essential constituent.

Should there be a deficiency of iodine in the diet, the

normal functioning of the thyroid gland is upset, which can have disastrous effects on the health.

The work of this gland is of the utmost importance because it regulates the metabolism of the body; that is, the continual chemical change that is going on whereby food is converted into energy, complex chemical substances are broken down into simple ones, and simple substances built up into complex ones.

The thyroid gland also regulates the energy discharge of the body, maintains its normal temperature of 98.65°F, and exerts an important influence upon all the other glands in the endocrine system. Once every 17 minutes the entire volume of blood in the body passes through the thyroid gland and becomes charged with its secretions.

The Cause of Goitre
A partial lack of iodine causes goitre, which is an enlargement of the thyroid gland. This enlargement is an attempt on the part of the gland to compensate for the lack of iodine and use the inadquate supply more efficiently. The gland overworks in trying to secrete more thyroxin than it has the ingredient (iodine) to do it with. The result is that it enlarges and causes pressure and fullness of the neck, which is a danger signal.

Goitre occurs frequently during adolescence when the body's need for iodine is greatest, and is much more prevalent among girls than boys.

Puberty, pregnancy, childbirth and the menopause are conditions that require more thyroxin than usual, and so the thyroid gland is often slightly enlarged at these times. After the emergency is over, the gland may decrease in size, or continue to grow, especially if not enough iodine is present.

Results of Goitre

In cases of simple goitre the gland may still manage to manufacture enough thyroxin to prevent visible signs of goitre, i.e., swollen throat, bulging eyes, etc., but there may be difficulty in swallowing, hoarseness, cough, and laboured breathing.

When, owing to a lack of iodine, the thyroid gland does not produce sufficient thyroxin, which contains about 64% iodine, the person becomes lazy, has no endurance, and puts on weight easily. Because of decreased energy the heart slows down, there is poor circulation, with cold hands and feet, lifeless hair that lacks lustre and falls out easily, and thin finger nails that split and break readily.

The memory is often faulty, owing to poor circulation of blood to the brain, and there are frequent headaches.

Lack of iodine may also cause the bone marrow to fail to produce enough red cells. Anaemia results, causing the fatigue to become intensified.

Recent surveys in America indicate that 40% of the women in many communities are suffering from the abnormally low production of thyroxin, leading to some or all of the above symptoms. There is no reason to believe that conditions are any better in Australia and New Zealand.

Thyroid Tablets

The usual treatment for this condition, which is commonly called 'thyroid deficiency' is to administer thyroid tablets containing thyroxin. These tablets contain the thyroxin taken from thyroid glands of sheep.

When these tablets are taken for any length of time, the thyroid gland becomes unable to carry out its normal function. In effect, it is enfeebled, like an arm that has been kept in a sling. Hence the use of thyroid tablets is not recommended except in cases where the thyroid gland has been surgically removed. Thyroxin tablets, under medical direction, are then essential.

Exopthalmic Goitre (Overactive Thyroid)

There is another form of goitre called 'exopthalmic' in which *too much* thyroxin is produced by the thyroid gland. In such cases all the bodily processes are speeded up. The heart beats too rapidly; the patient loses weight under the strain, becomes extremely nervous and suffers much from the heat. The eyes become prominent and protrude from their sockets.

Moreover, the food is forced so rapidly through the digestive tract that complete absorption does not occur, and the person becomes ill-nourished despite the food eaten. Such people find it impossible to relax because their nerves are in a state of continual tension, and unless they receive careful treatment, their complaint can prove fatal.

Need for Vitamins and Iodine

Quite apart from iodine, vitamins A, B-Complex, C and E are important for the proper functioning of the thyroid gland. A deficiency of these vitamins can cause a serious interference with the normal activity and output of the thyroid gland. This may give rise either to a sluggish, or an over-active thyroid gland, according to the constitution and inherited tendencies of the person concerned.

The thyroid gland requires approximately 0.1 milligram of iodine daily. The richest source of organic iodine is kelp, a type of seaweed obtained from the ocean. Tincture of iodine, prepared as an antiseptic for external use, *is a poison and should never be used internally*.

Goitre occurs naturally in certain localities where there is not enough iodine in the soil and the drinking water. These areas are known as 'goitre belts'. The prevention of goitre is a simple matter. Three kelp tablets contain sufficient iodine, if taken daily, to give immunity from goitre.

Goitre can also result from consuming milk from cows that have eaten certain weeds or grasses which prevent the thyroid gland from utilizing iodine in the diet.

Remedial Principles

The cure of goitre, whether it be caused by thyroid deficiency or an over-active thyroid, is a more difficult matter. In such cases what must be aimed at is to restore the thyroid gland to normal functioning. When the thyroid is sluggish, there is likely to be an anaemic condition associated with it, and foods rich in organic iron should be included in the diet. These are: apricots, prunes, dates, dried fruits, molasses, liver, parsley, egg yolk, and wheatgerm. The diet must be of such vital foods as fresh fruits and vegetables, lean meat, cheese and milk, eliminating the demineralized and refined foods that contain little nutritive value.

Vitamin Dosage

The following vitamins should be taken:

Before each meal: 1 Vitamin A tablet (750 i﹍
Vitamin B1 tablet (10 mg), 1 Vitamin B-c﹍﹍﹍
tablet, 2 Kelp tablets, 2 Calcium tablets, 1 Lecithin
capsule, 1 Vitamin C tablet (250 mg) and 1 desiccated
Liver tablet.

On retiring: 1 Vitamin B1 tablet, 1 Vitamin B-
complex tablet, 2 Calcium tablets, and 1 Vitamin E
(50 mg) tablet with a glass of milk.

ANAEMIA, SIMPLE AND PERNICIOUS

It is necessary to distinguish between the various types
of anaemia. Firstly, there is simple anaemia, due to
the lack of iron in the blood. Iron is necessary to
enable the blood to carry oxygen throughout the body,
and is of great value in helping to remove carbon-
dioxide from the tissues.

In a cubic millimetre of blood there are normally
over five million red corpuscles of red blood cells. The
number of these corpuscles varies widely with
individuals, depending on their state of health and is
spoken of as the blood count.

But apart from having sufficient red corpuscles,
each blood cell must contain a normal amount of
haemoglobin or red pigment, which actually unites
with and carries the oxygen. In all types of anaemia
there is a deficiency of haemoglobin in the blood, a
substance without which no one can live.

Haemoglobin contains organic iron in its
composition. The presence of this organic iron is
absolutely essential to life as it takes up the oxygen

brought into the system when breathing and carries it (in combination with itself) to all the cells of the body for their sustenance.

Haemoglobin gives the blood its red colour and a person deficient in this magical substance will have a much paler blood stream than one in good health.

Low Blood Pressure

But the anaemic person is not only pale and bloodless; *his blood pressure is low* and he is also without appetite and energy, because his impoverished blood is not supplying the vital organs and body structure with the proper amount of nutritional material, and so the whole organism, both physical and mental, is affected.

Let us deal with this important matter in more detail. The blood has been called the 'life stream' of the body. It is the means of transporting the digested food products from the digestive tract to all parts of the system, where they are stored in the liver, oxidized (burned) to produce energy, and used to renew tissue, bone, and tooth structure, and meet other bodily needs.

The Purpose of Oxygen

The body can only make use of this food material if oxygen is present, just as fire cannot burn without air.

The oxygen is carried from the lungs by the blood because the red pigment of the blood, called haemoglobin, unites with oxygen, as there is a strong affinity between them. When this oxygen-carrying pigment reaches the body cells it gives up its oxygen and receives in return the waste product, carbon dioxide, which is carried back to the lungs and is removed from the body in the expired air.

If, for any reason, the amount of haemoglobin in the blood is low, the blood cannot serve as a good oxygen-carrier and, in consequence, the whole body structure is improperly nourished.

Now, an essential constituent of haemoglobin is iron. If food iron is missing from our diet for any length of time, the blood pigment (haemoglobin) is weakened. This condition is known as nutritional anaemia and is characterized by paleness, listlessness and poor appetite.

Thus anaemia is not a disease, it is a deficiency condition, a state of bloodlessness due to improper nutrition.

It cannot be dismissed simply by saying, 'Ah, this person has anaemia. That means he is deficient in iron. What he wants is an iron tonic to cure him.' Iron tonics are made with crude, inorganic iron which is not well assimilated by the body. This kind of iron causes constipation and piles. It destroys the vitamin E in the system and gives rise to other undesirable side-effects. It is considered to be destructive to vitamin C.

Foods Rich in Organic Iron

Simple anaemia requires, in addition to the vitamins listed later, that the diet also includes iron-rich foods, namely: wheatgerm, yeast, raisins, apricots, molasses, parsley, egg-yolk, soyabeans, dates, dried fruit, liver, pumpkin, also prunes. The body is well adapted to assimilate the organic iron in foodstuffs, and iron in this form does not have an adverse effect upon the vitamin E in the body, or upon vitamin C, either.

Pernicious Anaemia

But there are more serious types of anaemia, called the macrocytic and pernicious anaemias.

Dr George Minot, of Boston, did a vast amount of research on these anaemias and found that the giant cells in the bone marrow were, for some reason, not manufacturing the red blood corpuscles. These giant cells in the bone marrow are called megaloblasts.

By a lucky chance, Dr Minot discovered that when pernicious anaemia patients were regularly fed on liver they improved. He then concluded that there was some factor in liver, the deficiency of which was the cause of the trouble.

Without it the megaloblasts in the bone marrow went on strike and the victim developed that waxy, yellow complexion, and lack of vitality bordering on prostration, that is so characteristic of this complaint. Dr Minot received the Nobel Prize for his twenty years' research into the problem of pernicious anaemia.

But the problem was by no means solved. People fed with liver got nauseated with it and indeed, became allergic to it. Science replied to this by developing a liver concentrate and injecting it into the body. But even this gave rise to allergies. The scientific research workers had long come to the conclusion that it was not the liver itself that effected the improvement, but something in the liver.

Disovery of Folic Acid

It was not till 1940 that they saw a gleam of positive hope. They found a vitamin in liver which they called 'folic acid'. They called it folic acid because it was also found in foliage, such as the leaves of lettuce and spinach.

Five years later, in August, 1945, a group of sixteen scientists in the employ of the American Cyanamid Company issued a statement, over their sixteen signatures, that they had succeeded in synthetizing folic acid. It was a momentous achievement.

The difficulty of obtaining folic acid from liver will be appreciated when it is realized that there is only one-tenth of an ounce of folic acid in *one ton* of fresh liver.

Professor Thomas Spies, whose amazing work in vitamin therapy is well-known, was on to the new vitamin like a shot. In November 1945, he tried it successfully on 26 cases of macrocytic and pernicious anaemia.

Now let us quote from Paul de Kruif's book on Professor Spies' work:

'It was out of this world the way this daily few milligrams of folic acid gave those reluctant, slow-downing megaloblasts a chemical kick in the pants so that they began pouring out reticulocytes – young red blood cells – in hundreds of billions out of his bone marrow into his blood; in a couple of weeks these wisps of crystals of synthetic folic acid gave him quarts of good, rich, red blood.

'It was epochal. Here was a new member of the family of vitamins that, for the first time in medicine's history, produced an effect on one of the most basic functions of the human body – blood building – an effect that you could count, that you could precisely measure, under your microscope, in exactly so many millions of red blood cells per cubic millimetre of blood.

'It was historic. About folic acid, Professor Spies

dared to write in superlatives almost never found in the drab chronicles of science. Within a year he had tested the yellow chemical's power on two hundred and seventeen anaemia cases. "The results," said Professor Spies, "were so incredible that time and again I could hardly believe my eyes."

'The news spread world-wide as a sort of sad little antidote to the earth's post-war misery and sorrow; and in the last few years observations by many scientists in many countries have confirmed the power of folic acid in many thousands of sufferers from macrocytic anaemias.'

Vitamin B12 for Pernicious Anaemia

We would emphasize, however, that folic acid does not cure *every* type of anaemia. There are types of pernicious anaemia accompanied by terrible nerve degeneration. In such cases, folic acid restored the blood count to normal, but did not seriously improve the nerve degeneration. But the scientific research workers were still burning the midnight oil – still trying one formula after another to wrest from liver another suspected secret that it held. And finally, in 1948, they succeeded. The magical vitamin – B12 – was isolated and manufactured synthetically.

The fact that no less than twenty tons of fresh ox liver must be processed to obtain only one gramme (a twenty-eighth part of an ounce) of vitamin B12 shows how important to anaemic people was the discovery that this vitamin can be produced synthetically.

Vitamin B12 not only does all that folic acid does, in manufacturing red blood cells to the normal requirements for health, but it remedies the nervous degeneration as well.

Vitamin Dosages

Dosage for simple (nutritional) and secondary anaemias:

1 Vitamin B1 tablet (10 mg), 1 B-complex tablet; 1 Vitamin C tablet (250 mg); 1 Kelp tablet, 2 Vitamin B12 tablets, 1 Folic Acid tablet and 1 desiccated Liver tablet, three times daily before meals. (All may be taken together.)

Dosage for pernicious anaemia:

1 Vitamin B1 tablet (10 mg); 2 B-complex tablets; 2 Vitamin C tablets (250 mg); 2 Kelp tablets; 2 Vitamin B12 tablets (10 microgrammes) and 2 desiccated Liver tablets, three times daily before meals. (All may be taken together.)

NOTE: If anaemia is suspected, it is always advisable to consult a doctor.

UNDERWEIGHT

While it is natural for some people to be thin and yet remain healthy, there is another kind of thin person who tires easily, is nervy, and who could add to his or her weight with considerable benefit to health. It is to this latter type that the following applies.

The problem of underweight is not solved merely by eating more food – it is much more complicated than that. Let us consider the reasons why people are underweight.

1. Some people worry at their meals which gives rise

to 'anorexia nervosa', or nervous lack of appetite. As the appetite dwindles, the sufferer continues to eat less and less. Meals should be eaten in a tranquil atmosphere, free from worry and bustle.

2. Then there is the person who eats 'foodless' non-vital foods just before a meal, thus replacing the more nourishing food served at meal times, for which he necessarily lacks appetite.

3. Some people lose interest in food because it is unattractively cooked and served. Such people will find that it takes some time to restore normal eating habits.

4. Purely mechanical causes such as bad teeth, sore gums, badly fitting dentures, ulcers in the mouth, and inflamed tongue (glossitis) can all cause a lack of interest in food.

5. The use of alkaline stomach mixtures and antacid powders, also sodium bicarbonate, will retard the secretion of hydrochloric acid in the stomach. This in turn gives rise to poor assimilation of food.

6. Some ailments, namely diarrhoea, colitis, dysentery, and sprue, interfere with the flow of normal digestive secretions thereby preventing the assimilation of food.

7. The regular use of toilet paraffin and other mineral oil preparations, prevent the absorption by the body of the fat-soluble vitamins A, D, E, F and K, and will result in malnutrition, manifested by loss of weight.

8. The use of sulpha drugs and exposure to X-rays gives rise to impaired liver function, thereby affecting the normal storage of glycogen, which is later converted into blood sugar and used for nourishing the body.

9. An over-active thyroid gland can as previously pointed out, speed up the entire process of digestion to the point where food is rushed through and out of the body before its nutriment has been properly extracted by the digestive system. This will cause underweight.

10. The regular use of laxative preparations can have the same effect as explained in 9 above.

11. People who are underweight are generally unable to relax. They hurry over their meals and jump up as soon as the meal is finished. This tendency must be overcome. The digestion should be helped by adopting a more relaxed attitude and resting for a few minutes after meals.

Calcium enables both nerves and muscles to relax.

According to Drs Bicknell and Prescott in their book *The Vitamins in Medicine*, underweight conditions in laboratory animals have been produced by depriving them of essential unsaturated fatty acids, otherwise known as lecithin.

Remedial Principles

Any lack of the B-group of vitamins, particularly vitamin B1 (thiamin) will result in poor appetite, flatulence and digestive disturbances after eating.

Underweight people generally require safflower oil, lecithin or sunflower seed oil capsules to overcome their shortage of unsaturated fatty acids. Such people can, with advantage, include more fatty foods in their diet, such as butter, cream and peanut butter.

Other vitamins which help those who are underweight are A, B-complex and C.

The following should, therefore, be taken three times daily before meals, all together:

1 Vitamin A tablet (750 i.u.'s); 1 Vitamin B1 tablet

(10 mg); 1 Vitamin B-complex tablet; 2 Vitamin C
tablets (50 mg); 2 Calcium tablets (white); 1 Safflower.
Oil, Sunflower Seed Oil or Lecithin capsule and 1
Kelp tablet.

THE HEALTH OF THE HAIR

Every living hair consists of a root and a shaft. The
root is embedded in a recess called a follicle, which is
surrounded by nerve fibrils. From the bottom of the
follicle there arises a small papilla, the growing point
from which the hair is pushed forward by continual
additions.

The hair follicle, papilla, nerve fibrils and hair roots
are all nourished by the bloodstream, hence it follows
that faulty nutrition must affect the hair adversely.
The colour of the hair is due to pigment granules
derived from the skin, and inadequate nutrition is
usually the cause of premature greying of the hair.

Every hair is provided with a small gland
(sebaceous gland) which secretes an oily fluid to
lubricate the hair and surrounding skin.

From the foregoing it will be realized that the hair is
nourished through its roots.

Falling Hair
Falling hair can result from infectious diseases, such
as typhoid fever, influenza, etc., also from the
administration of certain drugs such as thallium, tin
and arsenic.

In most cases of falling hair, however, defective

nutrition is the cause. When foods that are lacking in vitamins and minerals have been eaten for years, the bloodstream becomes toxic, and the hair glands and follicles are so impoverished that the hair is brittle and lifeless and eventually falls out. This is one of the causes of baldness.

Hair health depends upon bodily health, which in turn requires that our diet should be based upon such wholesome and *whole* foods as wheatgerm, unprocessed cheese, salad vegetables, eggs, fresh and dried fruits, nuts, milk, honey, brewer's yeast and molasses.

Fourth-rate foods and drinks are already dead and cannot nourish living bodies. They should be promptly eliminated from the diet. They include white flour products, refined white sugar, breakfast flakes and 'bubbles', salt, condiments, pickles and sauces, biscuits, jams, sweets, and soft drinks, synthetic cordials, polished rice, sausage meats, delicatessen products, fried foods, etc.; all of which are practically devoid of vitamins and minerals.

Research has shown that when vitamin A is under-supplied, the hair becomes dry, lacks sheen and falls out. Vitamin B-complex (which contains pantothenic acid) and vitamin C are also needed to maintain the colour, texture and vigour of the hair, together with kelp tablets for their iodine content, as thyroid deficiency is an important cause of lifeless hair.

Remedial Principles

Those whose hair is thin, brittle and unhealthy, should make the alterations to their diet already mentioned and also take the following vitamins three times daily before meals:

1 Vitamin A tablet (75 i.u.'s); 1 Vitamin B-complex tablet; 1 Vitamin B1 tablet (10 mg); 1 Vitamin C tablet (250 mg); 2 Kelp tablets and 1 Lecithin, Safflower or Sunflower Seed Oil capsule.

The scalp should be thoroughly massaged each night with the finger tips. When massaging, the finger tips should be dipped in a little olive oil or lemon juice, depending whether the hair is dry or greasy.

The hair should receive a good brushing night and morning, but care must be taken not to injure the scalp with hard bristle brushes, particularly nylon bristles, which are unsuitable for use on the hair and should be promptly replaced with hair brushes of natural bristles.

Greying Hair

Experiments with laboratory animals revealed that when fed on otherwise good diets, but lacking in certain of the B-group of vitamins, their hair began to go grey. When, however, these vitamins were added to their diet, their hair soon assumed its normal colour and growth.

Professor Adelle Davis, writing in *Vitality through Planned Nutrition*, states that dark-furred mice became grey when their diet lacked para-aminobenzoic acid, one of the B vitamins. Their fur changed back to dark again in two weeks after this vitamin had been added to their diet. A similar change in the colour of the hair was noted in foxes, black dogs and other animals.

Para-aminobenzoic acid is chiefly found in liver and brewer's yeast. Alternatively, a tablet of PABA (30 mg) should be taken daily.

Pantothenic acid, another of the B-group of vitamins, has been shown by tests on laboratory animals to be also necessary in preventing the premature greying of hair. It is one of the five vitamins contained in B-complex tablets.

Dandruff

The presence of dandruff in the hair indicates that the diet is lacking in vitamins. It is also evidence that certain unsaturated fatty acids, otherwise known as lecithin, are undersupplied. These fatty acids have a most beneficial effect upon the hair and skin.

Lecithin is contained chiefly in cereal and vegetable oils. Animals fats are an extremely poor source of supply. Sufferers from dandruff should take the vitamins already listed under Remedial Principles, three times daily after meals.

Anaemia

If loss of hair vitality is due to anaemia, it is advisable to add one folic acid tablet three times daily before meals, to the vitamins already mentioned. (See section dealing with Anaemia.)

Hair Washes and Scalp Lotions

A warning regarding the use of these preparations is given by Dr J.G. Downing of the Boston University School of Medicine, Boston, Mass., U.S.A. Dr Downing says that many chemicals are used that may cause trouble – the oils in bay rum; the synthetic perfumes in brilliantine; the various oils and resins in creams and 'wave' preparations.

Scalp lotions and tonics contain irritants and other substances that may injure the scalp. Shampoos contain perfume and various sulphur mixtures. Coconut oil shampoos are perfumed with several synthetic oils – any one of which may be harmful to individual users.

'Hair dyes and rinses are the oldest but still the most dangerous hazard of the hairdressers' trade,' says Dr Downing.

VARICOSE VEINS, VARICOSE ULCERS, THROMBO-PHLEBITIS

Varicose veins occur mostly in the legs and sometimes in the lower abdominal wall. The veins in the legs are the largest in the body and carry the used or de-oxygenated blood back to the heart.

If through wrong diet, constipation, lack of exercise or too much standing, these veins become enlarged, dilated or thickened and their valves weakened, the condition known as varicose veins follows. These veins are not only painful, but unsightly.

Varicose ulcers develop from varicose veins. If the skin in the lower part of the leg (in which varicose veins are present) is injured, the skin does not heal well and dermatitis may result.

Often the varicose veins cause itching, and if the skin is scratched a moist dermatitis may occur. This may become septic and healing is difficult. Eczema of the leg results, which frequently leads to ulceration, producing chronic varicose ulcers of the leg.

Blood Clots
Thrombo-phlebitis starts with the formation of a blood clot in one of the veins of the calf or foot. There is a feeling of pain and heaviness in the affected limb.

Obstruction of the vein may cause swelling. Thrombo-phlebitis may arise from an injury to the foot, but the toxic condition of the blood stream is the predisposing cause.

Great benefit will be derived in cases of varicose veins, varicose ulcers and thrombo-phlebitis by taking vitamin E, vitamin C, and lecithin. Vitamin E possesses an anti-thrombin quality, i.e., it diffuses blood that is already clotted and prevents blood clots from forming. Vitamin C builds strong connective tissue, which makes robust, healthy walls for veins, enabling them to cope with the flow of blood without weakening.

Lecithin

Lecithin is greatly deficient in the modern diet, and this lack is held by some research scientists to be partly responsible for the formation of varicose veins. The richest sources of lecithin are the cereal and vegetable oils, but many of these oils are nauseating. To obviate this difficulty a lecithin, safflower oil or sunflower seed oil capsule should be taken.

Remedial Principles

For varicose veins, one Vitamin E tablet or capsule of 50 mg, 1 Vitamin C tablet (250 mg) and one Lecithin capsule, to be taken before each meal.

For varicose ulcers and thrombo-phlebitis, the dosage of Vitamin E is two 50 mg tablets or capsules, or one 100 mg capsule, together with one vitamin C tablet of 250 mg, and one Lecithin capsule after each meal.

If there is high blood-pressure, only 2 vitamin E tablets or capsules of 50 mg should be taken daily for the first month, instead of six. Thereafter, the dosage should be increased gradually, as explained in the book in this series entitled *High Blood Pressure*.

A PROPER DIET

Practically all the people of the world feed badly, judged by the standards of the new science of nutrition; but the so-called civilized races feed worst of all, because so much of their food is refined, processed, cooked, embalmed, and its vital food value reduced or destroyed altogether.

There is, however, one oft-cited exception and it is worth the re-telling here since it serves to illustrate the point. This striking exception to the rule was discovered many years ago by Dr Sir Robert McCarrison, the famous dietitian, when he investigated the Hunza people living in the north of India.

He found that the people in this small province existed on a simple but sound diet and that all of them were in exemplary health. His report at the time said that their diet corresponded in many ways to that of the Sikhs, but that they ate less meat and, owing to their livestock being limited to goats, they consumed less milk and milk products. However, they were great fruit-eaters, enjoying plenty of apricots and mulberries which they ate in both the raw and sun-dried state.

The magnificent physical condition of the Hunzas was a source of amazement to McCarrison, and naturally he set about establishing exactly what it was that kept these people so fit and well.

He reported: 'These people are long-lived and

vigorous in old age. Among them the ailments too common in our own people – such as gastro-intestinal disorders, colitis, gastric and duodenal ulcer and cancer – are extraordinarily uncommon, and I have no doubt whatever in my own mind that their freedom from these scourges of modern civilization is due to three things:

'1. Their use of simple, natural foodstuffs of the right kind; 2. their vigorous outdoor life, and 3. their fine bracing climate.'

A Striking Contrast

Sir Robert McCarrison was impressed, as other observers had been before him, with the striking contrast between the manly, stalwart and resolute races in Northern India, as contrasted to the poorly developed, toneless and supine peoples of Southern India.

He found that the diet of the hordes about Madras, the diet that is the worst in all India, was based on rice which had been soaked and polished, thus removing most of the vitamins and minerals.

In *Health Via Food*, Dr Wm Howard Hay made the following commentary on the report of Sir Robert McCarrison:

'Numerous instances of longevity are reported from various quarters proving that men can, under certain circumstances, live to a much greater age than the usual span.

'Perhaps the most striking instance in recent times is furnished by Dr Sir Robert McCarrison, formerly of the British Army Medical Service, who reports that in a colony in the Himalayan region he found natives who were so old that it would be hard to believe their records correct, yet he was not able to detect possible errors in their way of keeping these records.

'Ages up to and well beyond a century were very common among them.

'He found men of well attested age up to 100 years and over recently married and raising families of healthy children.

'Men said to be well over one hundred years of age were working in the fields with younger men and doing as much work as any, in fact, looking so like the younger men that he was not able to distinguish the older from the younger.

'Beyond a small amount of milk or cheese, which were considered luxuries, the rest of the food consisted of grains in their normal state, nuts, vegetables and fruits.

'He reported that these people were never sick: they had none of the usual diseases of the civilized countries. They could not afford to cause them.

'There was, during his nine years' residence in this post, no case of indigestion, constipation, appendicitis, gastic or duodenal ulcer; no cancer, tuberculosis, kidney disease, gallstones, asthma, hay fever; he never heard of a case of cold or pneumonia or pleurisy.

'Is it possible that these people live so long and are so free from disease because they live very largely on the natural foods? . . .

'The largest mass example of longevity is that furnished by Sir Robert McCarrison, and surely comprises enough instances to make a sort of criterion that favours natural foods.'

What McCarrison Did

In his book, *The Wheel of Health*, Dr G.T. Wrench

wrote:

'Robert McCarrison qualified as a medical practitioner at Queen's University, Belfast in 1900. He entered the Indian Medical Service and sailed for India on his twenty-third birthday. He was posted as regimental medical officer to the Indian troops, stationed as warden to the frontier march of Chitral, between the Gilgit Agency on the East and Afghanistan on the West, in the heart of a country likely to prove one of utmost significance in the history of food. McCarrison had the inborn mind of a research worker. He quickly displayed it in the accustomed manner of medical research.

'In 1913 he was transferred to the Central Institute, Kasauli, with its well-equipped laboratories, and all that scientific colleagues and literature offer.

'In 1927 McCarrison was appointed Director of Nutrition Research in India under the Research Fund Association. He was not only director, he was, as he told the members of the Royal Commission on Agriculture in India, the only officer engaged on work on nutrition, so he had, as it were only to direct himself. He was given a laboratory and headquarters at Coonoor, upon the beautiful Nilgira plateau of the Madras Presidency, and there he directed his work and that of his excellent Indian assistants to the transference of the health of Hunza, Sikh and Pathan to experimental science.

'For this work McCarrison chose albino rats. Rats are largely used in nutritional laboratories. They offer many advantages for experimental work on foods. They are omnivorous and they like practically all human food. They are small animals and therefore cheap to feed. They breed readily in captivity, and their span of life is short, so that their whole life history can be watched.

'The first object of McCarrison was to see if the rats in their small sphere of life could be made exceptional in physique and health. He put them in good conditions of air, sunlight and cleanliness, and he chose as a diet for them, one based on those of the three peoples of excellent physique, the Hunza, the Pathans and the Sikhs.

Disease Abolished!

'The diet given to the rats was chapattis, of flat bread made of wholemeal wheat flour, lightly smeared with fresh butter, sprouted pulse, fresh raw carrots and fresh raw cabbage ad libitum, unboiled milk, a small ration of meat with bones once a week and an abundance of water, both for drinking and washing.

'In this experiment, 1,189 rats were watched from birth to the twenty-seventh month, an age in the rat which corresponds to that of about fifty-five years in a man. The rats were killed and carefully examined at all ages up to the twenty-seventh month of life by naked-eye post-mortem examination. The result was very remarkable. *Disease was abolished*. This astonishing consequence, however, must be given in McCarrison's own words in the first of two lectures given at the College of Surgeons in 1931.

'"During the past two and a quarter years there has been no case of illness in this 'universe' of albino rats, no death from natural causes in the adult stock, and, but for a few accidental deaths no infantile mortality. Both clinically and at post-mortem examination this stock has been shown to be remarkably free from disease. It may be that some of them have cryptic

disease of one kind or another, but, if so, I have failed
to find either clinical or microscopical evidence of it."

'By putting the rats on a diet similar to that of
certain people of northern India the rats became
"hunzarized", that is they "enjoyed remarkable
freedom from disease," words used by McCarrison in
1925 of the Hunza. They even went further. Except for
an occasional tapeworm cyst they had no visible
disease at all.

Diet, the Key to Health

'The only thing, therefore, that was common to rat
and man in this first experiment was the diet. Here in
the great cleft of Hunza was a little oasis of a few
thousand beings of almost perfect health, and here in
the cages of Coonoor was a little oasis of a thousand or
more albino rats also in perfect health. The only
connection between these two otherwise dissimilar
sets of living things *was a similar kind of diet*.

'McCarrison now linked up other batches of rats in
the same constant conditions of cleanliness and
comfort with other peoples of India by their diets. He
was in a most enviable position for trying out diets as a
whole. The Indian sub-continent provides so many
different races and different habits and diets. Hence
McCarrison was able to sit in his sanctum at Coonoor
and connect up his rats with teeming peoples near and
far, and in the mirror of the rats read the dietetic fates
of the peoples. He took the customary diets of the
poorer people of Bengal and Madras, consisting of
rice, pulses, vegetables, condiments, perhaps a little
milk. He gave these to rats.

'Now this diet immediately opened the lid of
Pandora's box for the rats of Coonoor, and diseases

and miseries of many kinds flew forth. McCarrison made a list of them as found by him in 2,243 rats fed on faulty Indian diets.

'The rats which were fed on the diets eaten by millions of Indians of Bengal and Madras, *got disease of every organ they possessed*, namely eyes, noses, ears, lungs, hearts, stomachs, intestines, kidneys, bladders, reproductive organs, blood, ordinary glands, special glands, and nerves. The liver and brain, it may be noted, do not occur in the list. The liver was as a matter of fact found to be diseased in conjunction with the diseases of the gastro-intestinal tract. The examination of the brain requires a careful opening of the small bony brain case of the rat and adds greatly to the time needed for post-mortem examinations.

'In a list given five years later in the Cantor Lectures, McCarrison adds a few further diseases such as general weakness, lassitude, irritability, loss of hair, ulcers, boils, bad teeth, crooked spines, distorted vertebrae and so on.

Remarkable Experiment

'In a later experiment, McCarrison gave a set of rats the diet of the poorer classes of England; white bread, margarine, sweetened tea, boiled vegetables, tinned meats and jams of the cheaper sort. On this diet, not only did the rats grow badly, but they developed what one might call rat-neurasthenia, and more than neurasthenia.

'"They were nervous and apt to bite their attendants; they lived unhappily together and by the sixteenth day of the experiment they began to kill and eat the weaker ones amongst them." We can add neurasthenia and ferocity to weaker brethren to the list.'

Disease is the Censor

'The effects of faulty feeding are not permanent in the race. They are not stamped into the race ineradicably by heredity. On the contrary, almost at a stride they could be abolished. Treat one generation rightly in the matter of food and bring and keep the next generation within that same correct feeding and the change would be effected.

'Meanwhile we know that the poor-European or poor-Madrassi-fed rat *is made the weakling that he is by the food he gets. His degeneracy is acquired.*

'Food is a condition – a primary condition – of environment. A good or bad condition of this environment is mainly dependent upon man himself. It is within his power to make almost miraculous changes.

'The prevention and banishment of disease are primarily matters of food; secondarily, of suitable conditions of environment. Antiseptics, medicaments, inoculations, and extirpating operations evade the real problem. Disease is the censor pointing out the humans, animals and plants who are imperfectly nourished. Its continuance and its increase are proofs that the methods used obscure, they do not attack, the radical problem.'

Dr James Empringham, the famous New York physician, has written:

'Most human beings automatically poison themselves. Not time, but the toxic products in the blood (due to improper nutrition and faulty elimination) produce the changes we call senile decay.'

Other recommended books...

LINDA CLARK'S HANDBOOK OF NATURAL REMEDIES

FOR COMMON AILMENTS

Linda Clark. Shows how to enjoy good health the natural way. Linda Clark is a leading reporter on health and nutrition and her book is a first-aid kit no one should be without—a thoroughly documented, easy-to-understand guide for all those who wish to take more responsibility for their own health and well-being. It covers many ailments, including allergies, anaemia, arthritis, asthma, backache, constipation, fatigue, headaches, indigestion, heart trouble and high blood pressure. In this book you will almost certainly find an effective new healing approach to whatever ails you.

LIVING MEDICINE

THE HEALING PROPERTIES OF PLANTS

Mannfried Pahlow. *8 pages of colour plates.* A guide to plants that have been scientifically proved to have healing properties. Shows how to recognize them, when to pick them, how to prepare them for medicinal use. All the plants and recipes have been especially chosen for use in the home, and are therefore perfectly safe if the instructions are followed exactly. *Includes:* The role of plants in modern medicine; The anatomy of plants; A catalogue of healing plants; The potent, the exotic and the new; Alphabetical home guide to common ailments and corresponding plant remedies.

MODERN HERBALISM FOR DIGESTIVE DISORDERS

AN ENCYCLOPAEDIA OF NATURAL HEALING

Frank Roberts M.N.I.M.H. Many years in the making, this book gives causes, symptoms, signs and curative prescriptions for digestive ills, including acidosis, alkalosis, appendicitis, constipation, diarrhoea, duodenal ulcer, gall stones, gastric ulcer, liver disorders and stomach troubles. Manner of presentation enables readers to find their ailments quickly and discover their exact treatment and prescription. An outstanding feature is a method whereby suspected diseases can be identified in their early stages. This is a truly comprehensive reference manual to modern practical herbalism for all digestive diseases.

INSTANT PAIN CONTROL

TRIGGER POINT SELF-TREATMENT

Leon Chaitow, N.D. *Fully illustrated.* How to locate pain 'triggers' in the body's soft tissue and apply simple self-treatment for easing pain throughout the body. Includes index of symptoms. If pain exists in an area listed there (or in the illustrations), search the appropriate trigger area for a sensitive spot, using thumb or index finger. Once identified as an active trigger, the point should receive up to one minute of sustained or intermittent pressure (or squeezing). This technique can dissipate headache, earache, sinus problems, eye trouble, abdominal pain—any postural, emotional and mechanical stress, or injury.